b small publishing

GRUESOME GRUB

AND

DISGUSTING DISHES

Susan Martineau
Illustrations by Martin Ursell

*With thanks for the idea to
Marta Fumagalli*

Published by b small publishing, Pinewood, 3a Coombe Ridings, Kingston upon Thames, Surrey KT2 7JT
© b small publishing, 1999
6 7 8 9 10
Colour reproduction: Vimnice International Ltd., Hong Kong. Printed in China
Editorial: Catherine Bruzzone and Susan Martineau *Design:* Lone Morton *Production:* Grahame Griffiths
ISBN 1 874735 45 X
British Library Cataloguing-in-Publication Data. A catalogue record for this book is available from the British Library.

Before You Begin

To get the best results from your gruesome cooking here are a few tips:

Once you've chosen a recipe it's a good idea to read it all the way through and get all your equipment and ingredients ready before you start. The recipes list exactly what you will need.

You should always have a grown-up standing by to help with any recipe steps where you need to heat food or use a sharp knife.

Keep some oven gloves handy, too, for recipes involving hot food.

Always wash your hands and put on an apron before cooking and make sure your work surfaces are nice and clean.

Afterwards...don't forget to wash up!

Unless otherwise mentioned, all the recipes serve 4 people.

All the spoon measurements are level ones unless it says otherwise.

If you use a fan oven please reduce the temperature by at least 10-15 degrees. You may also need to reduce the cooking time too.

Don't forget that all the ideas here are just to get you started. Have fun experimenting with your own creations too.

Beheaded Alien

A perfect pudding that is so easy to make, yummy to eat but looks really...yuk!

What you will need:

- 2 packets of jelly
- 6 marshmallows
- 6 x 14 mm lengths of dry pasta
- 2 liquorice whirls or 2 sweets
- measuring jug
- 1.2-litre heatproof bowl
- plate

Use slightly less water to make a firmer jelly.

1

2

3

Following the instructions on the packets, make the jelly. Pour into the bowl and put it in the fridge until set firm.

Dip the bowl in a sink of hot water for a few minutes to ease the jelly. Carefully turn it out on to a plate.

Push 3 marshmallows on to 3 pieces of dry pasta to create a tentacle. Repeat. Push into jelly. Position the eyes. Serve immediately.

Sick on Toast

A quick and easy snack and very tasty. Just close your eyes while you eat it!

What you will need:

- 4 eggs
- 100 ml milk
- salt and pepper
- 10 g butter
- 1 tomato, diced
- 1 slice of ham, cut into small pieces
- 1 cooked carrot, diced (optional)
- 4 slices of toast
- bowl and wooden spoon
- saucepan (non-stick)

1

Break the eggs into a bowl. Add the milk and beat together. Add salt and pepper to taste.

2

3

4

Melt the butter over a medium heat and add the egg mixture. Stir until the mixture begins to solidify. Keep stirring!

When the mixture is firm but not dry or burnt, stop heating and quickly stir in the tomato, ham and carrot (if using).

Spoon on to the pieces of toast and eat immediately.

Disgusting Dips

A selection of squidgy mixtures to dip into. You can dunk sticks of carrot, sweet red and yellow pepper, bread sticks, cucumber and crisps into the gunge.

Yuckamole

What you will need:

- 1 ripe avocado
- 2 heaped tablespoons cottage cheese
- 1-2 teaspoons lemon juice
- 1 tablespoon tomato ketchup
- salt and pepper
- knife and fork
- bowl

Peel and mash the avocado. Use a fork. Add all the other ingredients.

Serve immediately in a bowl. If you leave it, it will gradually look yuckier and yuckier!

Cement

What you will need:

- 250 g cottage cheese with pineapple
- 2-3 tablespoons cream cheese
- 6 green grapes, de-seeded and chopped very small
- 1½ teaspoons soy sauce
- some slices of toast
- bowl and spoon
- knife

Mix all the ingredients together. Add more soy sauce, if you like, to make the cement greyer.

Cut the toast into spades to serve with the cement.

Nasty Nibbles

These yucky lunch-time titbits can be made using muffins, baps, sliced bread or toast – whatever you prefer.

Mouse Trap

Half cut through a muffin or soft bap. Stuff with shredded lettuce and place half a hard-boiled egg inside. Mix a little mayonnaise with tomato ketchup and dribble this over the 'mouse'. Add a piece of cooked spaghetti or a strip of cheese for a tail. Be careful as you bite into it!

stuffed olive slices for eyes

cucumber slices for scales

strips of red pepper to make fishy lips

Fish Face

Drain a small tin of tuna and mix with a little Greek yoghurt or mayonnaise. Mix in some drained, tinned sweetcorn. Dollop on top of bread or toast and create your sinister fishy face.

cress hair

black olive eyes

Egg Head

Make a tasty troll face using a topping of finely chopped hard-boiled egg and cucumber mixed with mayonnaise.

cucumber lips and sweetcorn teeth

red pepper or tomato nose

7

Blood and Guts

This is a really filling supper dish with a deliciously gory sauce! Use a mixture of red, green and white spaghetti, rigatoni or pasta knots for a great gutsy look.

Keep the lid on the saucepan.

1

Heat the oil in the medium saucepan and fry the onion and carrot until soft.

What you will need:

- 75-100 g dried pasta per person
- 1 tablespoon olive or vegetable oil
- 1 medium onion, chopped
- 1 carrot, chopped very small or grated
- 400 g tin of chopped tomatoes
- pinch of mixed herbs

- salt and pepper
- 1 large and 1 medium saucepan (with lid)
- wooden spoon
- colander

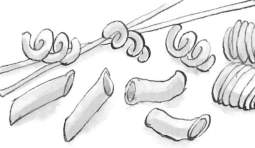

2

Add the tomatoes, herbs, salt and pepper. Stir and let it bubble gently, uncovered, for about 20 minutes.

Cook until the pasta is soft but still has some 'bite'.

3

Three-quarters fill the large pan with water. Add $1/2$ teaspoon salt, bring it to the boil, and add the pasta. Cook for 10-12 minutes.

4

Strain the pasta. Toss it in the sauce before serving. (This makes it look gutsier!)

Throat Throttler

A sinister drink that Dracula would be proud of. It's even got fangs to match. Try drinking while wearing them!

For each person you will need:

- 1 thick slice cucumber
- 1 glass cola
- 1 dessertspoon ice-cream (any flavour)
- knife
- tall glass
- 2 straws

1

First cut out your fangs from the cucumber slice as shown. You could try them on too!

2

Half fill the glass with cola. Add the ice-cream and then top up with more cola as it froths. Pop in the straws, decorate with the fangs, and serve.

For an extra fright you could drop in a lychee or two before adding the ice-cream. Use tinned or fresh, peeled ones. Just watch your friends' faces when they see what's lurking in their glasses.

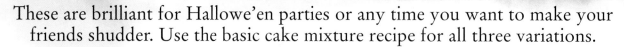

Creepy Cakes

These are brilliant for Hallowe'en parties or any time you want to make your friends shudder. Use the basic cake mixture recipe for all three variations.

Eyeball Cakes

What you will need to make 16-18 cakes:

- 100 g softened butter or margarine
- 100 g caster sugar
- 2 eggs
- 100 g self-raising flour
- 100 g icing sugar, sifted
- small packet of chocolate buttons
- red food colouring
- bowl
- wooden and metal spoons
- 18 paper cake cases
- bun tin
- cooling rack
- round-ended knife
- small paintbrush (clean!)

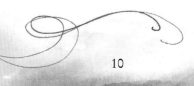

1

Cream the butter, or margarine, and sugar together until they are pale and fluffy.

2

Beat in the eggs, one at a time, with a tablespoon of flour with each. Fold in the rest of the flour with a metal spoon.

3 Cool on the rack.

Put paper cases in bun tin. Spoon in equal amounts of mixture. Bake in the oven at 190°C/375°F/Gas 5 for 15-20 minutes until risen and golden.

Mix the icing sugar with 1 tablespoon hot water until smooth and not too runny.

4

When cool, use the knife to cover the top of cakes with icing. Put a chocolate button in the centre of each. Using the brush, draw veins on the icing with red food colouring.

Bat Bites

Make chocolate cakes by using 1 tablespoon cocoa powder instead of 1 tablespoon flour.

Cut off top of cakes and halve the tops to make wings.

You will need some chocolate spread or chocolate icing. Spoon a small blob on to the centre, position wings and finish with silver balls for eyes.

Spider Sponges

Ice the cakes before decorating. You will need sweets of different sizes and colours.

black sweet for body

small sweets for eyes

liquorice lace legs

Snail Buns

You will need liquorice whirls with or without coloured centres.

Press liquorice whirl down on top of a thick layer of white icing. Don't worry if your snails don't hold their heads up ve...

Cut a slit down a whirl to make snail antlers.

Munch a Monster

A tea-time treat to give your family and friends a real scare.
Instead of making your own pizza bases you could buy ready-made
individual-sized ones from the supermarket.

What you will need to make 4 small monsters:

- 150 g plain flour
- 2 teaspoons easy-blend yeast
- 1 teaspoon salt
- 100 ml warm water
- 400 g tin of chopped tomatoes, drained
- 1 tablespoon tomato purée
- salt and pepper

- pinch of mixed herbs (optional)
- 1 large and 1 small bowl
- wooden spoon
- plastic bag, dusted inside with flour
- rolling-pin
- well-greased baking tray

Mix the flour, yeast and salt in the large bowl. Add the water and mix to a soft dough.

Knead the dough with floured hands for a few minutes. Put it in the bag and leave in a warm place for 15-20 minutes.

Dust work surface with flour.

Mix the tomatoes with the tomato purée, salt and pepper and herbs, if using. Divide the dough into 4 balls. Roll or press each one out into a circle about 16 cm across.

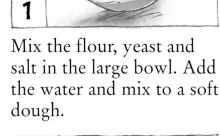

Place the circles on the baking tray and spread tomato sauce on each one. Add your toppings before baking at 200°C/400°F/Gas 6 for 20-25 minutes.

Let your imagination run away with you to create some really monstrous toppings. Sweetcorn kernels make horrible teeth. Layers of sliced courgette, pepperoni and stuffed olives make ghastly eyes. Use a slice of mushroom for a nose and make hideous hair out of yellow, red and green pepper.

Try cutting the dough circle into other awful shapes – like a skull!

Snot Surfers

A tasty bowl of slime soup topped with brave surfers.
Eat them quickly before they fall into the gunky depths!

What you will need:
- 1 medium onion
- 3 medium leeks, thoroughly washed
- 1 large potato, peeled
- large knob of butter
- 900 ml chicken or vegetable stock
- salt and pepper
- 4 slices of toast
- knife
- large saucepan with lid
- wooden spoon
- sieve (or blender) and bowl
- gingerbread man cutter

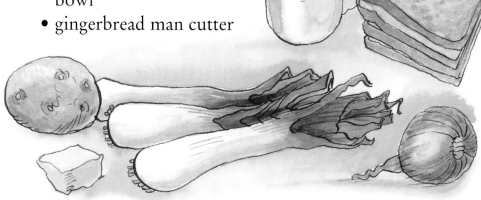

Stir occasionally.

1

Thinly slice the onion, leeks and potato. Cook gently in the butter for 10 minutes. Keep the lid on.

2

Add the stock and salt and pepper. Simmer for about 15 minutes. Then sieve or liquidize in a blender.

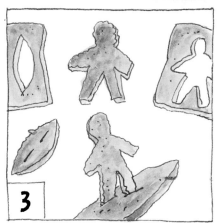

3

Cut out your toast surfers and their surfboards. Make slits in the boards and insert the surfers' feet. Serve one on each bowl of soup.

Slushy Slurps

Use as many different flavoured juices and cordials as you like to make these poisonous-looking, but definitely delicious, drinks.

What you will need:
- fruit juices and diluted cordials of your choice
- ice cube trays
- strong plastic bags and ties
- rolling-pin
- glasses and straws

blackcurrant

pineapple

lime

orange   lemon   apple

1

Pour the juices and cordials into ice cube trays. Put them in a freezer overnight or for a few hours.

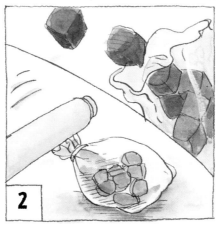

2

Pop the ice cubes out, one colour at a time, into a plastic bag. Seal the bag and bash the cubes with the rolling-pin to crush well.

3

Layer the colours as garishly as you like in glasses. Slurp through a straw.

Dead Man's Hand

A gruesome centrepiece for any party table, this will really revolt your friends and family. You need to put it in the fridge to defrost slightly before serving – just until the fingers wiggle!

What you will need:

- 1 large new rubber glove, very well washed
- 1 packet of yellow or orange jelly
- 1 packet of red jelly
- red food colouring
- red liquorice laces
- measuring jug
- jug and spoon
- 3 clothes pegs
- large plate
- scissors
- small paintbrush (clean!)

Make sure the jelly is well dissolved in the hot water.

1 Break the jelly into pieces. Place in the jug and dissolve in 300 ml boiling water. Then add 300 ml cold water.

You really need two people for this.

2 Over a sink, pour mixture into the glove and seal it well by folding over the opening at least twice and pegging it firmly.

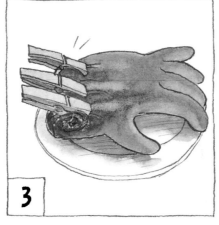

3 Place the hand palm side down on a plate. Space out the fingers. Put it in a freezer overnight.

4 Cut the glove, bit by bit, and gradually peel it off.

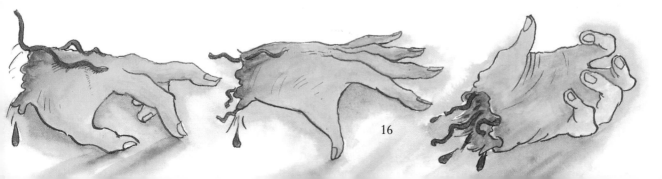

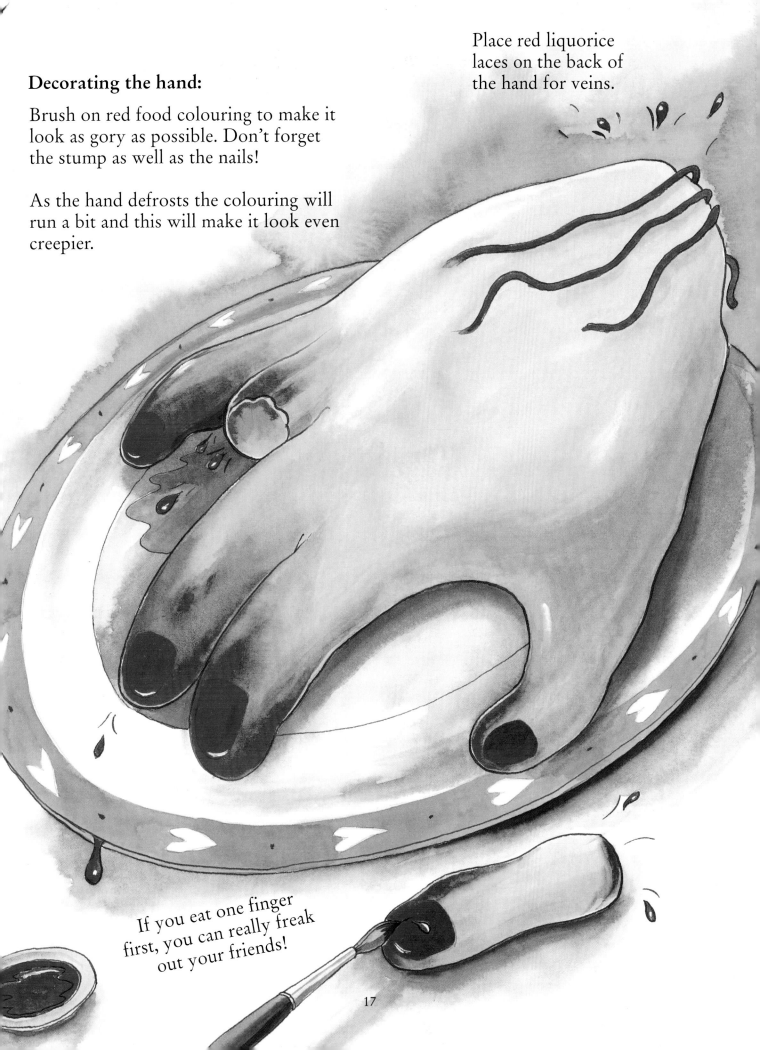

Decorating the hand:

Brush on red food colouring to make it look as gory as possible. Don't forget the stump as well as the nails!

As the hand defrosts the colouring will run a bit and this will make it look even creepier.

Place red liquorice laces on the back of the hand for veins.

If you eat one finger first, you can really freak out your friends!

Yeti Foot

A gory great foot which makes you glad the rest of the creature isn't around. Serve it with some salad or other vegetables for a complete monster meal.

What you will need:

- 4-5 medium potatoes, peeled, cut into chunks
- large knob of butter
- 50 g plain flour
- 1 egg, beaten
- 75 g Cheddar cheese, grated
- salt and pepper
- chunky chutney or tomato ketchup
- large saucepan
- potato masher
- wooden spoon
- greased baking tray

1

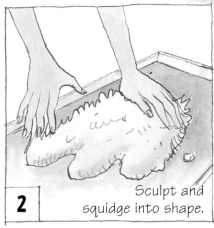

Sculpt and squidge into shape.

2

3

Boil the potatoes in a pan of water until soft (about 15-20 minutes). Drain them and stir in the butter. Mash until smooth.

Mix in the flour, egg and cheese. Season to taste. Place large blobs of the mixture on the baking tray in the shape of a foot with three toes.

Bake in the oven at 220°C/425°F/Gas 7 for 15 minutes until golden brown. Serve with the ketchup or chutney dribbled over it.

Bony Biscuits

These skull and bones biscuits are great fun to make. You could use red liquorice laces to tie some bones together. Don't worry if your shapes look a bit rough around the edges – they may have been buried for some time!

What you will need to make 18-20 biscuits:

- 150 g plain flour
- 75 g caster sugar
- 75 g butter or margarine
- grated rind of lemon (optional)
- 1 small egg, beaten
- a few raisins
- bowl and wooden spoon
- rolling-pin
- knife
- greased baking tray
- cooling rack

1 Use only your fingertips and thumbs.

2

3 Push in pieces of raisin to make nostrils.

Mix the flour and sugar in the bowl. Rub in the butter or margarine until it is like fine breadcrumbs.

Add the lemon rind, if using, and enough egg to mix to a stiff dough.

Roll out on a floured surface and cut out your skulls and bones. Place on baking trays and bake in the oven at 180°C/350°F/ Gas 4 for 10-15 minutes. Cool on a rack.

Maggot Cocktail

Invite your friends to try this squirmy starter – it really is delicious. It looks its wriggliest in glass dishes.

What you will need:

- 225 g cooked, peeled prawns (defrosted if frozen)
- 4 tablespoons mayonnaise
- 2 teaspoons tomato ketchup
- 2 teaspoons lemon juice
- pepper
- shredded lettuce leaves
- lemon slices
- spoon
- bowl
- 4 dishes
- greased baking tray

1

2

You don't need to be too tidy!

3

Serve with brown bread.

Mix together the mayonnaise, tomato ketchup and lemon juice. Add pepper to taste. Leave aside about 16 prawns and stir the rest into the mixture.

Make a bed of lettuce in each dish and spoon some prawn mixture on top.

Garnish with the lemon slices and remaining prawns. Make them look like escaping maggots! Keep in the fridge until ready to serve.

Whiffy Puffs

These look wonderful as they puff up and when you bite into them…phew! What a pong!

What you will need to make 8 puffs:

- 500 g packet ready-made puff pastry (defrosted if frozen)
- 40 g blue Stilton
- 1 egg, beaten

- flour for dusting
- rolling-pin
- 7.5 cm round cutter
- pastry brush
- baking tray
- knife

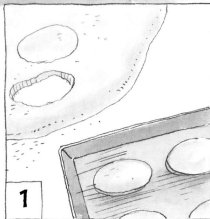

1

On a floured surface, roll out the pastry until it is 4-5 mm thick. Cut out 16 rounds. Place 8 on the baking tray.

2

Put a knob of Stilton in the middle of each. Brush the pastry edges with egg. Place the remaining rounds on top. Press down and pinch the edges firmly.

3

Cut a small slit in each top. Brush on some more egg and bake in the oven at 220°C/425°F/Gas 7 for 10-15 minutes. Serve hot.

Cowpat Pudding

This looks disgustingly like the real thing but is a really moreish treat. If you want to add texture to your cowpat you can always mix in some dried fruits like raisins or glacé cherries with the biscuit crumbs. Yum! Yum!

What you will need:

- 225 g plain wholemeal biscuits
- 100 g butter, cut into pieces
- 100 g plain chocolate, broken into pieces
- green sweet laces
- a few raisins

- large plastic bag and tie
- rolling-pin
- mixing bowl
- 18 cm round cake
- cooking foil
- small saucepan
- wooden spoon

1 Put the biscuits in the bag. Seal, and crush into tiny crumbs with the rolling-pin. Empty into the bowl.

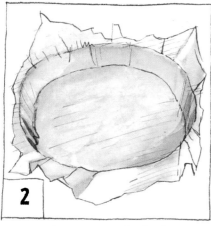

2 Line the tin with foil, making sure it goes right into the edges.

Make sure all crumbs are coated.

3 Put the butter and chocolate in the saucepan and heat gently. Stir until the chocolate is melted. Pour into the biscuit mix.

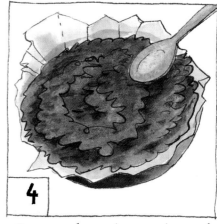

4 Spoon the mixture into the tin. Press it down and use the back of the spoon to make circular patterns on top. Put the cake in fridge to set for at least 2 hours.

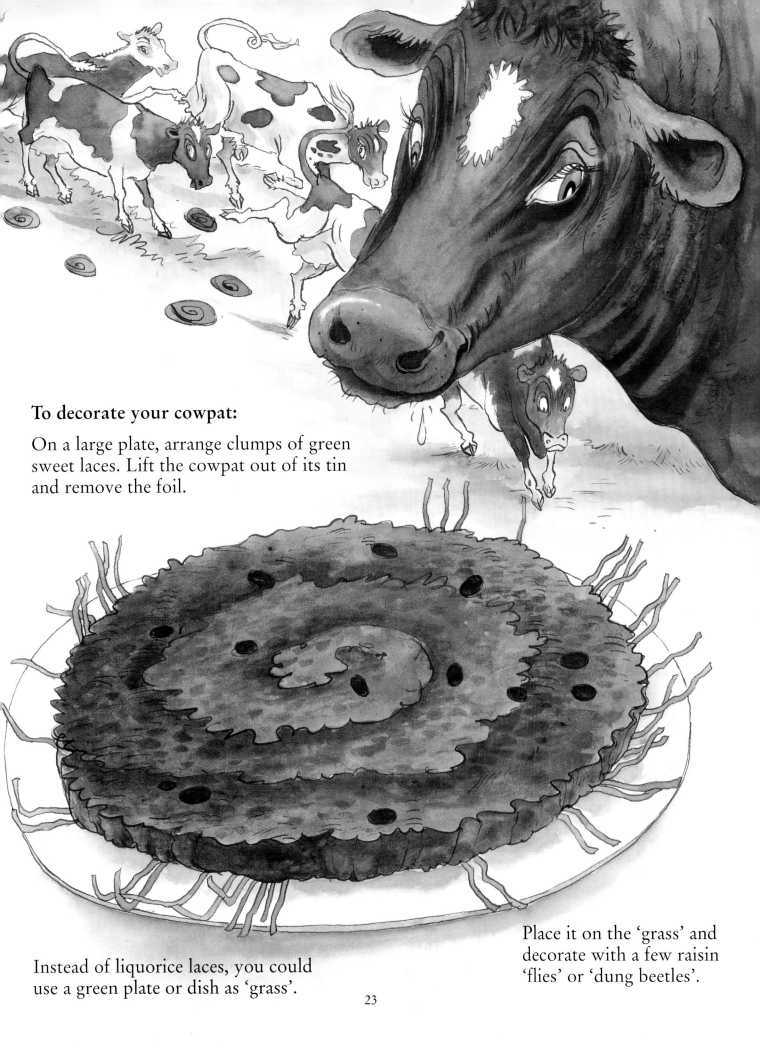

To decorate your cowpat:

On a large plate, arrange clumps of green sweet laces. Lift the cowpat out of its tin and remove the foil.

Instead of liquorice laces, you could use a green plate or dish as 'grass'.

Place it on the 'grass' and decorate with a few raisin 'flies' or 'dung beetles'.

23

Axeman's Snacks

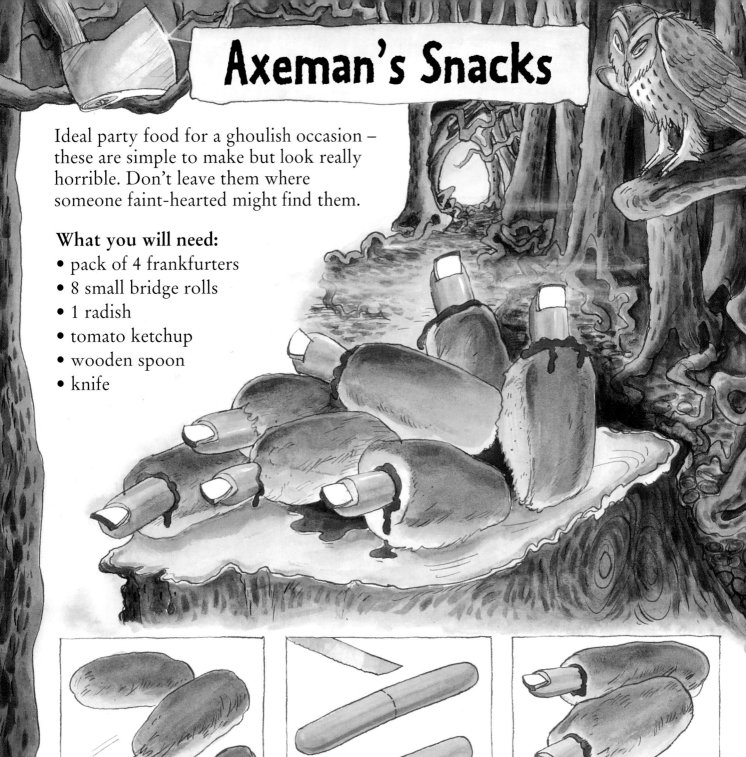

Ideal party food for a ghoulish occasion – these are simple to make but look really horrible. Don't leave them where someone faint-hearted might find them.

What you will need:
- pack of 4 frankfurters
- 8 small bridge rolls
- 1 radish
- tomato ketchup
- wooden spoon
- knife

1 Use the handle of the spoon to push a hole almost all the way through each roll.

2 Spoon a little ketchup into each hole. Cut each frankfurter in half and then cut a 'bed' for each nail in each closed end.

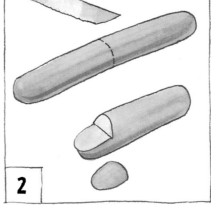

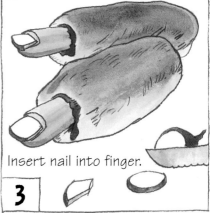

Insert nail into finger.

3 Push half a frankfurter into each roll. Cut a thin slice of radish and then a wedge from this. Trim to make a nail.